Afternoons Go Nowhere

In memoriam Dalpat Ram

Afternoons Go Nowhere

Sheenagh Pugh

Seren is the book imprint of
Poetry Wales Press Ltd.
57 Nolton Street, Bridgend, Wales, CF31 3AE
www.serenbooks.com
facebook.com/SerenBooks
twitter@SerenBooks

ISBN: 978-1-78172-498-9
ebook: 978-1-78172-499-6
Kindle: 978-1-78172-500-9

A CIP record for this title is available from the British Library.

The publisher acknowledges the financial assistance of the Welsh Books Council.

Cover photograph: © Phil Cope.

Author photograph: © Sam Burns.

Printed in Bembo by Latimer Trend & Company Ltd, Plymouth.

Contents

Sacking the Palace of Savoy

London, June 1381

No looting was allowed. Walter said,
*we are not thieves. Samson did not pocket
the temple vessels.* We had never handled

such stuff. I saw men lay velvet
to their cheeks, stroke silk with fingertips
before their knives ripped through it.

We beat the silver cups
into uncanny shapes; they fell
at our feet, grimacing up

like pained faces. And the jewels…
so many, such rich colours.
We ground them all

into flinders. The whole floor
was a shingle strand.
We bruised price, crunched glitter

underfoot. We opened our hands,
working men's hands, over the Thames,
and emptied coin. Then we burned

the palace down. I still dream
the ashy tang. Yes, one fellow
stole a goblet. We drowned him;

nothing else we could do.
Poor man, he was tempted.
We understood. But we too

were poor. We needed
the honour of that day:
it was all we had.

The Glass King of France

When he looks in the glass, he sees
himself: every organ, every vein.
His most inward thoughts shine
through his crystal skin; the secrets
of his heart parade the streets,
bold-faced, flaunting. Nothing of him
but is open to view. He could die of shame,
yet he walks gingerly, in fear

of the chance knock that could shatter
a king to fragments. Raised eyebrows, smiles
behind hands; no one credits how fragile
he is, except his enemy, advancing
from the coast, God's own chosen king
with his blank, unreflecting eyes.

The Byzantine Emperor's Entry Into Paris

June 1400

On a white horse (borrowed)
and poorly attended,
the Emperor Manuel Palaeologos
rides into Paris.
He eyes his hosts sideways,
pricing their jewels
and guessing how large a loan
they might be good for.

This city is bursting
beyond its walls, building
so high, its jutting roofs
elbow out the sun.
He thinks of Constantinople,
shrinking year by year
into less space, as if
the Turks might pass it by.

The King who gives him
the kiss of peace
makes a fine figure
as they ride together.
The French nobles breathe easy:
it's one of his good days.
He won't lean over
and whisper to his guest,

I'm made of glass, you know;
I might shatter any moment.
His mind spends months
in the dark: one day,
there for good, he will recall
the summer of the Emperor
who rode beside him, looking
so well, so carefree.

Isabelle is

Isabelle is a daughter   France's daughter
king's daughter   daughter of a war
four times as long as her life.

She is a bride-price   a ransom
six hundred thousand ecus cash down
she is eleven.

She is a mother   three sons
who might as well be nameless
and Valentina.

Isabelle is who   la princesse de France
la comtesse de Vertus   la duchessa
di Milano.

Isabelle is where   Paris
Pavia   Milan   palaces   gardens
the Visconti vault.

Isabelle is not   is cold
is a memory   a name   unmade
she is twenty-five.

Isabelle's daughter the duchess   her grandson
the great poet   her great-grandson
the king.

Isabelle invisible   inscribed
in family rolls   a footnote
to histories.

Behind others   always behind others
indistinct   guessed at   Isabelle   slipping through
white space.

Ça Ira

It'll be fine, it'll be okay,
they sang as they swung on down the road
to make the world work a better way.

Freedom, equality, brotherhood,
everyone's dream, how could it fail,
once they'd cleared out the dead wood.

Only the axe was under a spell,
chopped and chopped and never let up,
like something out of a fairy tale,

and when they finally made it stop,
nobody had any appetite
for freedom; no one could handle hope.

It'll be fine, it'll be all right,
except that for now they've all slunk back
to where they were, or maybe not quite.

Perhaps just a small step down the track
can make a difference next time they try;
perhaps every ship that goes to wrack

is wood for a better. It could be
that men become wiser, that they shun
the evil they know, that history

is the tale of progress. Then again,
they might be like the vomiting cur
from the Bible. Yet… it'll be fine,

they sing, after every ruinous war,
each tyranny, pogrom, disastrous choice.
The axe chops on, till they remember

the magic words: poll, armistice,
uprising. Then they hand out freedom,
give folk doctoring, schooling, a voice,

welcome strangers into their home,
seeing their brothers. Though they turn
again to their folly, still it would seem

there's something in them that longs to learn,
that gropes for light, yet flinches away,
loving the glow, fearing the burn.

It'll be fine, it'll be okay,
freedom, equality, brotherhood,
it'll be fine, just not today.

The Offering

There was a sea-cliff, they say, where fowlers
inched down ropes, stepping on air, to steal
birds' eggs, and they say an ancient evil
lived in the rock. A grey hand would seep out,
reach for the rope that held the life and cut.
At last comes Bishop Thorlak to bless
the face of the rock, each outcrop and crevice,
taking it back. He is almost done,

when a voice, toneless, hollow, as if stone
could speak, breathes out of the cliff:
"The wicked too must have somewhere to live."
And the good Thorlak, nodding, leaves one slope
unblessed, unclaimed by man, a death-trap
for all but gannets, puffins and cliff-monsters.

The Monk and the Margin

The most holy saint, both before and after her death, performed many notable miracles; would that the warming of this scriptorium had been among them. I trace gold letters with blue, numbed fingers. It is reported for a truth that roses would spring up where she walked. My window is etched with frost-flowers.

Little devils apply toasting-forks to the toes of the damned. A flying dragon blows the winter forest from white to red.

She had taken a vow of chastity and, being threatened with marriage, embarked with fifty maidens in a small boat, in which they fled to preserve their virtue. Which the LORD approving, brought them through many storms to an island, where the boat was wrecked, but them He saved alive, and untouched of man.

Among the waves do fish and dolphins and all the creatures of the sea couple with such joy, they leap from my pen.

On this island was no sustenance, nor had they the means of fishing, but the LORD caused great shoals of fish to leap from the sea, and the stones of the beach became hot, so that they were cooked as they landed. So too caused He a dead tree to grow heavy with all manner of fruit. Today is a fast day. My head is light; I am so empty, I could fly.

A fox wheels a barrow of apples. Two eagles bear between them in their beaks a spit, upon which a sheep roasts. A drunken hog lies under the running spigot of a wine barrel.

There came a king, a heathen, with his men, and would have attempted their virtue, whereon they fled into a cave. When the king would have followed them, they prayed to the LORD and He caused great stones and rocks to fall in the mouth of the cave and stop it up. Thus could not the king come in, nor the ladies go out, and they starved in the dark cave. I have lived in this house since boyhood. My eyes are webbed from overmuch copying. It seems to me the LORD could as well have caused the rocks to fall on the heads of the king and his men, and left the cave open.

Green vines curl about my capital; they burst into bud and the flowers open into butterflies. An elephant gambols upon the rainbow. Above the wave, a whale opens his mouth and the little silver fish stream out like larks and rise into a golden sky.

Time Zones

1. Eastern Time
Montreal, Quebec

They built a gracious habitation,
but it looked back, looked eastward.
The old-world houses, the boulevards
named for kings and saints, the kind
of life they'd gladly left behind
for the new, for chance, elbow room,
a space where history and custom
were theirs to make. Yet they were nostalgic
for a world of Protestant versus Catholic,
French fighting English, aristos flaunting money,
mansion vaults in the very cemetery.
We may both be dead but you're still poor.
How long does it take, I wonder,
to let go, to prefer the unknown?

2. Central Time
Somewhere in Manitoba

God knows where this is:
nowhere different from ten miles
back or forward. Fields like skies,

flat green or gold the fill
of a window, a sightline.
It's all a matter of scale;

nothing wrong with green
in little, but maxed-out
it goes beyond human,

like the road, dead straight,
that marches further
than eyes can follow. The thought

of walking that road, never
a bend or hill, knowing always
what's next... They've a saying here:

watch your dog run away
for three days – though where to
is a question, and why,

in this vastness where somehow
hours and days become words
and there's nowhere to go.

3. Mountain Time
Jasper, Alberta: Canada Day

Fossils from ocean's floor
embedded in the mountains

that rose so slowly, slower even
than the Athabasca Glacier

inching toward the Arctic.
How long does water take

to scoop a hollow in limestone;
how many centuries go

to a full-grown pine? Today the mayor
spoke of difference, celebrating

the variety of humans
in his small town surrounded

by immensity. In the shadow
of so much time, doomed lives

leave marks on rock, chip away
at ice, make moments count.

4. Pacific Time
Vancouver, British Columbia

Go far enough west,
you end up east:
the city by the Pacific
tastes of miso and lemongrass.
Australian accents
sound on streets whose signs
are painted in characters.
In the park, Arden's forest
takes shape with a cast
of all the world's actors.
Palms among pines,
a confusion of scents:
salt, patchouli, grass.
A port's a place of traffic,
of meeting. *East*:
so close, so nearly *west*.

A New Psalm of Montreal

with apologies to Samuel Butler

Rue St-Paul early, sunlight trickling down
the tall stone buildings to warm cobbles
and flagstones damp from overnight cleaning,
or stabbing with sudden warmth from side-streets:
oh morning, oh Montreal.

Too early for the homeless man and his cat
with its diamante collar and sleek black fur,
too early for the pubs, the pavement cafés,
the street stalls, the girl with the violin
who plays to Montreal.

When we cleared customs, the nice man checked
our return tickets, I suppose in case
we planned to stay, drop off the radar
in some laid-back, sunny, bilingual spot
like St-Paul, Montreal.

And it is sounding like a fine notion,
now that the snivelling wet little island
whence we came has stumped off, doolally, muttering
to itself "You'll all be sorry when I'm gone".
Oh dear: oh Montreal.

And St-Paul is waking, drinking its coffee,
watering its hanging baskets, setting out
its goods: sun is drenching the walls now
and a terrible guitarist is tuning up:
oh summer, oh Montreal.

A slim girl with the very slight swell
of early pregnancy swings smiling by,
dropping coins in every cap on the pavement,
and I would quite like to apply for asylum,
oh please, oh Montreal.

Departure Bay

There's a bus to Departure Bay,
it leaves on the dot.
You could get there easy enough,
but better not:
what place in the world could live up
to a name like that?

As long as you never go
to Departure Bay,
it will smell of engine oil
and wood and salt spray;
and boxes and bales and crates
will be piled on the quay.

Travellers waiting to board,
that light in their eyes,
checking their tickets again,
postponing goodbyes,
wondering what they've forgotten
and whether it matters.

What if you go, and find only
a commonplace town,
thrift shops and trumpery goods,
buildings run-down,
a vague reek of burger bars
and desperation?

For this is the surest thing
about adventure:
the only place it can happen
is in the future,
and the best of a journey is never
after departure.

The Islanders

They came first for the fishing. Cleared just enough
woodland for summer shacks. Got to like it:
shored 'em up, stayed the winter. Trod paths
through the sand. In great-grandfather's time.

Peaceful place, long way from City Hall,
who left 'em mostly alone, back then.
Just a couple of islands no one else
had a use for. 'Fact, when they moved folk

out of the way of the new airport,
they floated their houses over here,
on rafts, I think. That was before the war.
There was maybe two thousand lived here then.

A whole neighbourhood. Even rich folks;
they had the mansions beside Lakeshore,
where the boardwalk is now. All along,
you can see foundations, stone walls crumbling.

Bulldozed, the lot. For an island park,
they called it, like a zoo or a playground.
But inland, the old wooden houses
held out, though trees and bushes inched

round them, like camouflage. Because from then,
- fifties, sixties - they had a fight on their hands
to live where they called home. In the way
of developers, city plans, the future.

They only clung on by calling themselves
history. Sorry, *heritage*. Tourists take snaps
of ivy fingering windows, gateways
almost hidden, gardens going back.

They talk to a man who lives in the house
his grandfather built, and ask how he manages
without shops. Yeah, the exhibits are safe,
but then there's the kids, they look over the water

at the bright lights. What's left to them
they'll leave, as like as not, to the holiday trade.
You see some old guy, just about staying
on top of roof repairs and a wilding plot,

and you wonder if he wants it that way,
for the woods to walk gently in at the door,
between the planks, up though the floorboards,
taking back what was never given.

Distant Canadian Wildlife

Moose is a dark solidity
at the lake's far edge,
a brown unexpectedly rich.

Wolf steps shyly from a stand of pines,
delicate as Agag, dreaming of deer
and the bitterness of death.

Redwing blackbird flashes
his epaulets in flight,
then folds into sobersides.

All are momentary: none
will come close or stay long
while you get your camera.

Some just cross the edge
of your eye; you will never
be sure you saw them.

You see what you see: fix it
or lose it. This is the way
things are meant to be.

Ronald

(Lord Cardigan's horse)

Ronald galloped
to where the noise came from,
then back again.

They always want you to go
toward the noise.
Mostly, more come back.

Some horses break,
lie screaming, thrashing
in the smell of blood.

Or their man breaks
and they stay by him,
nuzzling his face.

Ronald came back,
like one in six,
he lived to be old.

When his man broke,
Ronald was to walk
behind the coffin

but stepping so slow
and with no man
set him on edge

and the laudanum
they used to calm him
made him doze off

(against a wall,
let's hope, like Marvin's horse
in Cat Ballou).

Someone sounded
the cavalry charge
in his old ear: it pricked,

and he paced with the guns,
the music, left his man lying
and came back.

The Moon…

i.m. Dan Leno, 1861-1904

1.

The music-hall stage is backed with mirrors:
the child, his act over, turns unthinking
into the glass. The impact jars

his whole body. He sits stunned, shaking
his head, hearing laughter. The audience
take it for stage business. They're egging

him on: do it again! Applause
aching, echoing, waves of love incarnate.
Seeing stars: a star. Heading, in a trance,

for the mirror. When someone asks: are you hurt,
he slurs in wonder: *yes,*
I am, but didn't they like it!

2.

The moon was in its usual line of business,
strolling through the streets of heaven,
while the audience tried, helpless

with mirth, to follow a Dan
gone manic, breakneck. He'd rattle
down the tram-track of unreason,

dodging everyday objects turned feral:
cakes show *an extremely obstinate nature*
and *there's something awfully artful*

about an egg. When he finally careers
off-course, they'll clap to bruise their hands.
The moon whistles The British Grenadiers.

3.

Laughter is the sound of friends,
the echo of success, the proof
you're still in the mirror. If it ends,

you die. No one can get enough
who has once heard it, not him,
for sure. What doesn't raise a laugh

may as well not be. *What is that atom*
of bar-loafing clay called man? What is he for?
A snug, a ward, digs, a dressing-room,

too narrow, all, for an explorer
of cloudcuckoolands. What if no one clapped
and all the windows turned to mirrors?
"The moon," he started. *There he stopped.*

The italicised phrases in this poem are direct quotes, some from Leno's stage act,
others from "Dan Leno, Hys Booke".

Oral English

Ichigoro Yuchida, keen to improve
his colloquial English, puzzles over

a text with his (equally baffled) teacher.
They can't seem to find *dolly old eek*

in the phrasebook. And why, during a shipwreck,
should Mr Horne laugh when our heroes

drag themselves up on deck? So many queries…
in the end, they think best to seek wisdom

from the writer, which is how they come,
courtesy of Mr Took, to knowledge

of some comic stereotypes, a secret language,
a national habit of wryness, a way of talking

as if one could make a joke of anything,
of code, of hiding from the law, of love.

Airline Pilots

The way they talk, that level tone,
lazily amused, a refusal

to be surprised, that seen-it-all,
been-there-done-that air: no pose,

too easily worn. It calms the nervous,
of course; maybe laid-back gets learned

in training, the last wavering notes ironed
out of the voice before they graduate.

But it sounds more like the kind of secret
that makes one smile the more it's hoarded,

to do with living the blue side of cloud,
above the toy landscape they keep leaving.

In sudden earnest, they might hear themselves saying
I am acquainted with the sun.

Afternoons Go Nowhere

Butter hardens in the dish overnight:
the tourist office keeps winter hours.

The year's last cruise ship has left the harbour
and the voices of Italy, New York, Japan,

are heard no more in the street. Afternoons
go nowhere. Dark falls early, finds folk

up ladders, spades in earth, work
unfinished. Radiators cough into life:

plumbers and sweeps can't find light enough
to get round, clear out the debris.

Somehow no one is ever quite ready
for this, as if they half hoped

time too would let things slide, be up
some ladder finishing what started late.

La Catalana

Port St Julian, Patagonia

In Port St Julian a house once stood,
well known to men in the neighbourhood,

the kind they call a house of ill fame,
and yet it bears a noble name.

Consuelo lived at La Catalana
with Maud, Amalia, Maria, Angela,

and every night they worked, in their way,
like the men who tilled the fields all day.

But back in 1922
the bosses were driving wages low,

men got no good from all their work,
so they downed spades and went on strike.

In came the Army to save the state
from folk demanding enough to eat,

and General Varela's troops, quite soon,
had fifteen hundred neatly mown down.

Killing peasants can be a chore;
the soldiers fancied some R & R,

so the conquering troops of General Varela
marched off to unwind at La Catalana.

Consuelo went to fetch a broom
and swept the rubbish out of her room.

Angela prodded them down the stair,
Amalia pushed them out at the door.

Maria said, as she slammed it shut,
"We knew the men you bastards shot.

Some were our fathers; we caused them shame,
but we sent them money all the same.

Some came for comfort, their muscles aching;
this is one strike you won't be breaking."

And English Maud from the window shouts
"Murderers, get out and stay out!

Go back and tell General Varela
how you couldn't storm La Catalana!"

Well, the police were called, and ran them in,
so, when they all got out again,

their names were on record: Maud, Amalia,
Angela, Consuelo, Maria,

who will be honoured as brave and good
as long as language is understood,

which goes to show, as any can see,
that words are tyranny's enemy,

as is comradeship, the sense to know
who your friends are, when to say no,

and there are times nothing hits home
like an angry woman with a good broom.

The Winchman on Oscar Charlie

I'd like to be the winchman on Oscar Charlie,
if I weren't afraid of heights and helicopters:
lift people lightly from a pitching deck,
head through the dark to Christmas-blazing oil-rigs,
see from high up, so often, I'd almost forget
to take notice, porpoises leaping, the shadows of orca.

I met his mother-in-law at a bus stop once,
the winchman. She told me his working day
you wouldn't believe, the things he'd seen and done,
when now and again she could make him talk about them,
but there was the rub. He wasn't a talking man;
he was strong, fearless, fantastic head for heights,

and he could have filled volumes with the way
he lived the world, the betweenness, sea and sky,
land, deck and platform, that rope, danger and safety,
if he knew the words that would make them happen
for the likes of us, checking our shopping lists,
wondering why the 9.20's late again.

Sensory Acquisition

His sight failing, he gazes
toward a distant church.
White tombstones uproot themselves
of a sudden, galloping
flatfootedly to the man
with the feed bucket.

Speak of paracetamol; he hears
Paris in turmoil. A tame housecoat
slips its peg, prowls the shadows,
an ocelot. The world
in his ears grows more various,
less commonplace, by the day.

Memories richer, more detailed
the further away. Was his life
really like that? Words, acts
tumble-polished till the beach
is a stretch of light,
a perfect story?

Hoswick: Winter

In the fields
>more geese than sheep

in the bay
>more seals than boats

in the sky
>more night than day.

The Painter's Bored Husband

Enthusiast, she was out in all weathers
painting seascapes from the cliff path.
He was faithful; they'd been years together,
often doing what pleased them both,

sometimes following each other's whim.
If, late in life, she'd a fancy for oils
and canvas, that was all right by him:
he'd tag along, carry the camp-stools,

chew patiently on a grass stalk
while art happened. There'd be birds to see,
the odd rabbit. Walkers would stop to take
a breather, pass the time of day.

When she got stuck on a fiddly bit
and hours went by like weeks, he began
to build things. Loose rock lay all about;
his first effort was a small cairn

the wind scattered, but he got the hang
of filling in gaps, strengthening corners:
he'd plenty of practice. It wasn't long
before he was leaving stone signatures

wherever they'd been, and his handiwork
has lasted; long ago the old couple
passed on, but tourists on the cliff-walk
still pause, photograph, wonder which people

from ancient times, going the same road,
stopped off to craft, with such loving intent
and in honour of which vanished god,
this trail of small enduring monuments.

The View

For as long as he could remember, the view
from his window had led across a street
to some house the mirror of his own,

and what he could hear through the double-glazing
mainly traffic, heels clacking on asphalt,
late at night, a little drunken happiness.

Now he looks out on a bay, cuts his hedge
hard back, ruthless with the white roses
that would come between him and the ocean.

The nearest houses are over the water,
scattered among fields, few and single,
each built to its own pattern.

To the south is a grove of sycamore
iridescent with starlings, sibilant
in the salt wind. He is waiting for winter,

for trees empty of leaves and birds,
cupping only light and the open sea
between their bare branches.

The Wrong Way

North wind resists the tide, pushes it back
from the beach in long lines of herringbone
that shiver the sunlight. A blue bright, broken
everywhere with silver, but never a wave
nor a sound, or none that can live
against the wind. No frills, no can-can lace
kicked up into brief rainbows, no voice,
just a sea going the wrong way,

a drawn-out, glittering goodbye,
as it seems, though muscles under its skin
tense, maintaining the ground, holding on
for the wind to change, to help it rush
the shore, shout, spend itself, go smash
in the sheer joy of its attack.

The Man Who Disliked Crocuses

My neighbour had a dislike of crocuses,
though he loved gardening. The leaves

were a mess; hung about too long,
he said, after flowering.

His wife died of a lingering illness:
he'd loved her, as far as I could see,

brought heart-shaped stones from the beach,
painted them white, propped them against the house.

He went to pieces a bit, afterwards,
rehomed his rescue animals,

found a flat in town with no garden.
I'd still see him, now and then,

hanging around outside the bookie's;
he'd ask after my cats, my rock plants.

A lesser man, but still a wit,
edged like the green blades that break

winter ground. He'd a way to go, yet,
to ruin the leavings of his life.

In the court report, his age surprised me:
I'd have guessed him ten years older.

So much life left, so little point;
and every spring, they come back.

It's true they die hard and untidy,
but John, one could pardon so much

for those few days when sun
opens them full, their given time.

Visitor

Sometimes, after a storm, sand shifts,
stones are flung aside, and a skull
stares out, or a framework of ribs
startles with its whiteness. Whole villages
have come back: hearths, stone tables,
even the shelves built into their walls.

Captured then, before they could resume
the skin they left on the rocks, they live
in our light, all their arrangements,
oil lamps, loom weights, open, like a bombed house,
its front wall gone, forced to display
carpets and wallpapers to public view.

The one nearby, though, was more slippery.
A layer of rock slid away from a shape
two thousand years old; it was photographed,
but the cliff lurched again and took back
this brief acquaintance, the neighbour who called in
just once, and whom we never got to know.

Bus Station

Passengers on the move, not moving,
becalmed in a between place

on the way elsewhere. Dead quiet, staring
intently into their palms.

They are talking with their quick fingers,
eyes flickering, picking up messages,

catching the latest news. They know
the price of gold, what's happening in Iran,

tomorrow's weather; they scan the world,
their faces backlit; they are no spectators

but part of the play, tuned in
to a global exchange where thoughts,

facts, rumours, insults zip along wires
like cash on a Baldwin Flyer. It's off-key,

this silence; it should hum, crackle
with static; we should hear a buzz

pitched just too low for eavesdroppers,
the sound this glow would make, that wells

from a dozen tiny screens
into the room whose windows

are dark with winter, looking out
only on our own reflections.

Quarff Gap

A place named for nothing,
a nothing, a space
in a spine of hills,

a great scoop of sky
in a green spoon, a doorway
from east to west.

A place with a past
before history started.
Think the river back,

the giant whose bed
you stand in. It would run
where the skuas balance

between two hills,
where air pours
in place of water.

Something was here,
now nothing is. Nothing
fills the eye,

bowl-shaped, windblown,
the colour of weather,
salt-flavoured, singular.

Who knew nothing
could be such a landmark?
From the North Sea,

sailing up this coast,
bays blur; nesses flatten out,
it's hard to tell

townships apart.
But no one can miss
the gap, the emptiness

that signs its name
across landscape, sky,
that draws the fancy

like a window, or rather
the space in a ruined wall
where a window was.

Rules of Conversation: Hoswick

Unless actually raining, it is a *fine day*
and must be remarked on, lest the gods
of weather, affronted, take the sun away.

All objects, except boats, are masculine:
shears, watches, nails. *I dunna mind*
where I left him, but he's no' workin'.

Don't ask where people live. *It's where*
do you stay? Our tenancy
in the world is a transitory matter.

The Maid of Norway Window

Lerwick Town Hall

Softness itself, the fair hair loose,
flowing over fur, the childish curve
of the cheek. And metal: one crown
heavy on the small head, her hands
full of another. Her cloak clasped
with a gold breastplate, massive pearls
weighting the six-year-old neck.

The little plush doll who set sail
in autumn gales to cross the North Sea
for reasons of state. By the time
they made Orkney, she was wrung out
like a rag: dry-lipped, hollow,
bruised with retching, she slipped untimely
from the diplomatic grasp

and stands now in glass, most fragile
of hard surfaces, light flooding through
her skin to fall on the faces below,
men discussing money, ordering matters
as they see fit, managing small lives.

Head Gulls

King Edward the Seventh postures on Union Street
looking ridiculous in granite breeches.
The sculptor, we see, has done his best to imbue
the florid features with an unmerited hint
of nobility; has disguised the little paunch
in the folds of a stone cloak, but all is undone
by the republican, bolshie, sarcastic seagull
perched on his head.

It is the same, praise be, all over Scotland:
wherever a statue stares over folk's heads
with that trademark, costive sublimity,
there'll be a seagull cackling in his curls,
on his helmet, his mitre, his Stewart cockade,
his poet's laurel. Great men all, pose as you please
in bronze and marble, you'll find no man is a hero
to his seagull.

Seagulls are atheists, anarchists, troublemakers
to a bird, lower-deck mutineers, sea-lawyers
with a salty, raucous laugh. They don't do deference
or fan-worship; they are strangers to decorum.
If they were comedians, they'd be Max Miller;
if they were instruments, they'd be kazoos.
If they were characters from history,
they'd be the jester

with his fool's licence, waving a pig's bladder
in the faces of the mighty; they'd be the slave
who rode with the moment's Caesar in his triumph
muttering, "You're still going to die,
you know that?" For every oration, may there be
a satirist; for every emperor, a small boy
with sharp eyes, and may every statue be crowned
with a seagull.

Lieutenant Schmidt's Ideal Lady

1. The Lady at the Kiev Racecourse

A new century not long begun:
a young man, unhappily married
and between trains, is at a loose end
on a sultry Kiev afternoon.

He goes to the races: sees a lady
in the crowd, the most beautiful lady
imaginable. Her black eyes, her hair,
the darkest night flowing like water.

He thinks she might be Spanish; he pictures her
on a warm shore he has only seen
from the deck of his ship. She is swept away
on the tide of racegoers; he never meets her,

never hears her voice. This does not displease him:
he is a man who lives in fancy
and will simply love her for ever.
That night, he takes the train to Sevastopol.

2. The Lady on the Night Train to Sevastopol

Now you must know, the train was lit by candles
held in lanterns, as the manner was,
and they swayed so with the wheels' rocking,
the carriage was all fitful, shifting shadows.

But a woman stepped in, and he glimpsed
by the guttering light the face from the racetrack;
he was sure of it. He told her his love:
she was married, of course; she would be,

but then so was he, and virtuous.
They talked in the dark, exchanged names and addresses,
then she got off half an hour down the line
at Darnitsa. Back on his ship, he writes her

letters like love poems, tells her his dreams
of freedom, revolution, a new country.
Hers to him are in prose, everyday gossip
on commonplace matters: this he never notices.

3. The Lady Who Came to Ochakov

Waiting for the firing squad, the Lieutenant
begs his sister (who would rather spend
what time she can with him than go
on a fool's errand) to fetch The Lady.

So she is found, and even her husband
urges her to the journey, so loved
is the Lieutenant. And she comes to him,
and when she enters his cell, he pales,

because the woman on the night train
is not, after all, the racecourse lady,
the one and only. He sees a housewife,
no great wit or beauty, a good heart

who has come a long way in winter to comfort
a man's last hours. He steps forward
and holds the realness of her, the human warmth
that does what it can against the dark.

The facts behind this poem are related in "Southern Adventure", vol 5 of Konstantin Paustovsky's autobiography "Story of a Life" (pub. in English Harvill Press 1969, tr. Kyril FitzLyon)

Guests at Frodriver

It started in autumn with a dead shepherd
who didn't rest easy. He loomed up
in a doorway, scared another man
to death; the widow pined away,
then a farm-hand fell sick... And each one,
dying, joined the company.

Around Advent, the master and six hands
went out fishing and never came home –
well, not alive... Come the funeral feast
they all walked in, reeking of salt, sea
pouring from their clothes, and sat down
by the fire. While they were still steaming,

in came the land-ghosts, shaking soil
from their shrouds, the earth-smell hanging
strong about them. We living folk
thought it time to decamp to another room,
leaving them the fire. That Christmas,
the dead were warmer than the living.

It was a lawyer and a priest showed us
what to do. We held a court: summonsed
each one. They came up in their turn,
dripping seaweed or worms, listened quietly
as we sentenced them to be banished
for ever. And as each left the fire

for the door, he spoke. One said, I recall,
"I've stayed as long as folk would let me",
another, "I'm going now, and it seems
I should have gone sooner". And then they walked
out into winter, truly absent at last,
and we could almost have called them back.

Imperfect Knowledge

Young Eirene in the great bed of state,
almost lost among silks and brocades,
holding her triumph, her first son,
heir to the eastern empire, who will be
her only child, though the bustling ladies,
the unctuous courtiers, the smiling father
do not know this: still less, that mother and son,
two decades hence, will fall out over ikons.
Eyes screwed shut, his small face nuzzles
to the warmth of the body he has known
these nine months, and her arms respond,
tightening around her hope. And if she knew
she would come to love power too much
to let it go, and if he knew that she,
one day, in this room, would depose him; order
his eyes put out, if they both knew,
even then, it would not change this moment.

A Roman Tombstone at Annaba

My name was-
What does it matter? – Paulus Silentiarius

It would happen so easily. The harassed mason,
busy elsewhere, leaves a small job of lettering
to his journeyman. Nothing elaborate,
no bigwig's lengthy encomium; the master
would have seen to that himself. Five words,
a modest inscription for a modest stone.

And besides, what could go wrong? The fellow
is a good hand enough, and he has only
to follow a template. Which he does,
exactly, so that his master, returning,
reads, chiselled clear and strong into the stone,
HIC IACET CORPUS PUERI NOMINANDI.

"Here lies the body of the boy [Insert
Name Here]". The mason is first speechless,
then all too voluble, but when he has cursed
himself calm, he admits the fault was his:
he should never have assumed the man could read
those shapes his eye followed so faithfully.

And now, what is to be done? A spoiled stone,
even so humble a one, is a heavy loss.
His clients can read Latin no better
than his craftsman; what they need in their grief
are the magic marks that say, at least to them,
that someone missing was once here.

Can it even be said he is cheating them,
he wonders: does the stone not rather,
by these words, this space, leave the dead boy,
who was no one of note, level with the city's greatest,
the heroes of old? He claps his flustered workman
on the shoulder. There is no harm done.

The Joy of Five

The death mask: wax and plaster
and living clay
that follows the man's indents,
his scars and furrows,
that makes him eye us sideways,
still grave and worried
after five hundred years,
as who should say:
to bring the dead alive, my dear,
to bring the dead alive.

Then the plates, the paper,
the silvered film
where the latent image seems
to swim from nowhere.
They call it a likeness, this inch-tall
man who can neither move
nor speak. It is what character
comes to: what else will serve
to bring the dead alive, my dear,
to bring the dead alive?

It was cinema said "action",
get up and walk,
gave the voices back
to folk long gone.
What would Andrew Marvell
say, to see years speed by
in time-lapse? Maybe
"Now make it stand still".
What brings the dead alive, my dear,
what brings the dead alive?

Bodies have been frozen
in vaults, loved pets cloned,
(they say a cat's markings
are never the same twice).
But loss knows no reason;
none so alone
as the bereaved, so ruthless:
they will try anything
to bring the dead alive, my dear,
to bring the dead alive.

A man in Dorset hands
a wife only he can see
into a cart; talks, all the way,
to the void at his shoulder.
The space where someone was,
the gap of light
between the bare branches:
hold on to that.

The Centenaries

January 2017

Three years now they have been trudging by,
grimy and fading, staring straight ahead
as if they did not see us: Ypres, veiled
in poison gas, Marne with its fleet of taxis
ferrying men to death, meters running,
Gallipoli leaving its dead abandoned
with the other debris on the beach,
Loos in its coat of barbed wire hung
like a shrike's larder, Mametz Wood,
not a tree standing. The latest was Verdun,
a sunny day blazing on the Pals
from Accrington. Passchendaele's coming up,
very slowly, dragging feet, hooves, wheels
from the sucking mud. It will pass close
for a moment, then dwindle into distance
after the others. And when the Armistice,
all flags and gravestones, has had its moment
and tramped off into the dust-cloud,
they'll close the road, rename it "history"
and forget the names on its signs,
the changed landmarks, the stories discarded
unfinished all along the way.

Some Rocks Remember

"I consider induced rocks to have Alzheimers. They are the rocks that forgot where they were born and how to get home" – Prof. Suzanne McEnroe, Norwegian University of Sciences and Technology, Trondheim

Some rocks remember where north was
when they were formed. The poles wander
about the world, and you can track
their paths in haematite, magnetite,
that answer no compass, because they carry
the printout of how things used to be.
Remanant, they are called; they don't change
with the times.

                The others, the less constant,
realign themselves, fall into step
with the magnetic field, reflect the now,
the new. The knowledge of where they began
is gone, or buried where they can't come at it.
Geologists name them *induced*: liken them
to minds with Alzheimers: *the rocks that forgot
where they came from and how to get home.*

But surely it is the mind familiar
with old magnetic paths whose compass fails,
who cannot find home now, for thinking
of home that was. They have their own north,
those remanants; we all do, and when
the world's north alters, there's our needle
true to the errant pole, still pointing
to Abyssinia or Van Diemen's Land.

The Border

The border is the river
but a river moves, turned aside
by pebbles, its puzzled banks learning
to speak new languages. Or the border
is that mountain range, shouldered
upward when two continents clashed –
you can still find fossils, seashells
from the ocean floor etched
in its ridges. A fence marks the border:
it follows the line of an old field-wall
robbed from the stones of a ruined fort;
the dip beyond was the ditch, once,
of a causewayed enclosure. The border
is reshaping itself, unseen, as it has
since earth hardened. It shifts
all the while the short-term tenants,
guarding the ground they call their own,
scowl across the wire, measuring
the distance a bullet need go
to end a brief stay sooner.

The North Wind

If I had known my eyes would web over
I would have stayed awake
as long as light.

I would have gone out in all weathers,
learning to tell trees apart
and the pathways of stars.

The world is full of places
I never went to:
once they were destinations.

I have photos of people
who aren't here any longer.
I wish I had videos,

but I could never get the hang
of making videos. The people
in the photos have lost their voices:

they went out in the north wind
and their faces, so quick,
so mobile, froze

in one attitude:
talk and joke all you like,
they won't smile back.

Their accents are fading, flattening out.
I would have listened harder
if I'd known that would happen,

if I had known about the north wind
and the passage of time.
But you did know. You knew

all of that, always.
I can only say
that was not how it seemed.

The more of age, the nearer

The moyr of age, the nerer hevenes blisse – Robert Henryson

He yearned, as a young man, to go into space,
shed the magnets that kept his shoes anchored,
float free of earth. But the chance never offered
until he was old. Now he would begrudge
missed sunsets, woodsmoke, a whole March
without celandines. His view narrows, sharpens
each year, homes in on detail like the lens
of a microscope. *The more of age, the nearer,*

not to heaven; that's neither here nor there,
but to what is in plain sight
and always was, the earth beneath his feet
that now, even for a day, he would not leave
before he must: no, not to have
the run of all the unnumbered galaxies.

Seascape with Dying Author

Dieppe, 1870

He is old; his day is past,
he is done with writing.
At his son's house on the coast
he sits resting, waiting,
a guest with time to waste
staring at nothing,

so they think, but there they mistake.
It is December:
the light falls angled and weak
on the pebbly shore,
touches the chalky rock
and flickers over

the hems of the creaming waves.
It is the sea
he watches: the danger that moves
under its skin, the way
it homes in, the way it leaves
without saying goodbye.

He fills his failing eyes
with ocean and winter light;
frost in the air catches
the back of his throat
but nothing escapes his gaze
till the tide goes out.

Only the day after
his death will the Prussians march in,   .
almost as if they feared,
while he lived, that the swordsmen
with their plumed hats and rapiers
might rise up, young again,

from the place in his mind
where he kept the matter of fancy,
still bright, still destined
to be the enemy
of the dull, the disciplined,
and scatter their army.

Liverpool Alexandria

If they had stayed in Liverpool,
if the business had prospered… They say
he spoke Greek, all his days, with that edge
of strangeness.

It was a seaport, after all,
like the other: he could have followed
his fancies down different streets, loitered
in Victorian pubs heavy with gilt and brass
instead of the pavement cafes.

It is not as if he were one for road names
or landmarks. His city was not made of weather,
knew no seasons. Its map was people: Cleopatra,
shop assistants, Coptic priests, Lefkios
and Iasis, flaneurs, emperors, debauchees,
all crowding in, on every corner an Antony.

It could have worked, in that city of Welsh chapels
and Chinatown, that importer of languages.
He could have written the epitaphs of so many:
slaves, sailors, emigrants, chancers, young men
going to seed… it would have been just like home,
would have *become* home.

A life mapped out in one city, he said,
would follow the same contours anywhere:
we'd have had him, the quiet stroller,
bringing folk in the Walker back to life,
haunting the Philharmonic, locking eyes
with lounging shadows in Gibraltar Place. Already
he'd made the odd poem in English; soon enough
it would have become his music, shaped his thought,
even if he spoke it, always, with a Greek lilt.

In the Land of the Dead

CREON: The good and the bad are not equally deserving.
ANTIGONE: Who knows? In the land of the dead they may be.
– Sophocles: Antigone

Now and then, a mind turns a corner
or tops a hill, and the view is what
it never dreamed of, the world so *other,*

it is thrown off course, can't see straight,
or rather, it sees for the first time
that straight is not what it had thought.

Walls and horizons, nothing is plumb
but all aslant. It is how the girl sees,
for a moment, past the narrow room

where we step round each other, set laws
to ease our time together. It is sound:
it renders our life civil. But her eyes

have opened on the endless land beyond,
with its soaring valleys, its plunging mountains,
its lack of signs and frontiers: the land
where all the maps are to draw again.

The Healer

Meden agan, he says, in the hollow voice
of a reed-pipe: all air, all music,
and the florid king, face of the sun, is struck
at table, falls forward, rich sauce dyeing
his silks. His poet, numbed, is trying
to believe in the end of the story
he was in: *he was here yesterday*.
Sometimes the arrow does not kill
but leaves a half-life: no taste, no smell,
everything slowed, colours bleached out.
Too much world can over-excite
the senses. The god watches the man
struggle to speak; leans in. *Meden agan*,
Apollo whispers: *nothing in excess*.

Wher beth they, bifore us weren?

For it is impossible for anything to come to be from what is not, and it cannot be brought about that that which is should be utterly destroyed
– Empedocles

Seeded in the dark, it hankered for sky:
it shouldered beyond the forest shade
to touch sunlight. Under an axe
it became a house, a boat, a book,
lived a new life, fell from use
to kindling: the fire caught and blew it
to flinders that flew and cooled to ash.
Or it crashed and rotted, eaten with age,
into earth, under it, stifled, pressed
beneath lifetimes, ice ages, until it hardened
into diamond or anthracite.

And the poet who riddled it took a pen
from a greylag's wing that had flown oceans.
He made ink of oak-galls, rust, rainwater
and he laid his words on a calf's skin
that ended its days as a kitchen rag.
Then he fell, he too, back to earth,
leaving his song in the ears of many,
hoping that they, before the air
forgot their voices, would throw it on,
like a ball that passes from hand to hand,
never falling.
                        Should it console us somehow
that what looks so like annihilation
is only change? That beaches were cliffs,
that coal was once leaf, that flesh and bone,
even, become humus and lime
to feed new life? If this is comfort,
why does our breath catch, our heart turn over
when a dead man is lifted from permafrost
or peat bog with his face still on,
looking as if you could shake his shoulder
and wake him?

We've no cause to love change,
that's the truth of it. Surely something
is lost; surely a body is
not just limbs, but their running lightness,
not eyes only, but what lit them,
and where does that go, Empedocles,
what becomes of it?
                    The ball passes
from hand to hand, but its colours
fade in the sun: one day, perhaps,
it drops in the grass, lies half hidden,
its purple weathered to grey.

And it may be a poem, so perfect
it lives on the page or tongue
for long ages of men,
but it may be no more
than a neighbour's good nature,
a workman's craft, a joker's quick wit,
and these are soon gone, as soon
as the last man dies
who kept them in mind,
yet they *were*, as surely as cliff and leaf,
but where is the sand, the coal
that came of them?

Is there a beach somewhere,
unmapped, unvisited, whose sand
was ground from the soft stone
of all that has slipped from mind?
Could we run through our hands
the grains of a girl's longing,
an artist's gift, a palaeolithic jest?

Show me the sand, Empedocles,
show me the sand.

Acknowledgements

Some of these poems have previously appeared in *Agenda, Ambit, Black Light Engine Room, Double Bill, High Windows, InterlitQ, New Boots and Pantisocracies, Poetry Nation Review, Poetry Spotlight, Scotia Extremis, The London Magazine, The New Welsh Review, The New Shetlander, The Stare's Nest.*

SEREN

Well chosen words

Seren is an independent publisher with a wide-ranging list which includes poetry, fiction, biography, art, translation, criticism and history. Many of our books and authors have been on longlists and shortlists for – or won – major literary prizes, among them the Costa Award, the Jerwood Fiction Uncovered Prize, the Man Booker, the Desmond Elliott Prize, The Writers' Guild Award, Forward Prize and TS Eliot Prize.

At the heart of our list is a beautiful poem, a good story told well or an idea or history presented interestingly or provocatively. We're international in authorship and readership though our roots are here in Wales (Seren means Star in Welsh), where we prove that writers from a small country with an intricate culture have a worldwide relevance.

Our aim is to publish work of the highest literary and artistic merit that also succeeds commercially in a competitive, fast changing environment. You can help us achieve this goal by reading more of our books – available from all good bookshops and increasingly as e-books. You can also buy them at 20% discount from our website, and get monthly updates about forthcoming titles, readings, launches and other news about Seren and the authors we publish.

www.serenbooks.com